How to Create Effective Content on the Web

Practical Guide

G. Dellis

Copyright © 2024

Guide on how to create effective web content

1.Introduction

The importance of effective content to attract online interest cannot be underestimated in the digital age we live in. With so much online competition, it is essential to create unique, interesting, and relevant content to capture your audience's attention and keep your readers engaged. In this article, we will explore how to create engaging online content for a business or blog, with practical tips and strategies to follow.

1. Know Your Target Audience

Before you start creating content for your blog or online business, it is essential to have a clear understanding of your target audience. Who are your ideal readers? What are their interests, problems, and needs? What do they look for when browsing the internet? This information will allow you to create content that resonates with your audience and generates engagement.

You can obtain this information using demographic and behavioral analysis tools like Google Analytics or Facebook Insights, conducting online surveys, or directly interacting with your followers on social media. Once you have identified your target audience, you can create targeted content that meets their needs.

2. Choose Interesting and Trending Topics

When it comes to creating engaging online content, it is important to choose topics that are relevant, interesting, and trending for your target audience. Monitor current trends in your industry and try to create content that is timely and in line with the latest news. You can use tools like Google Trends or BuzzSumo to identify popular topics and understand what is capturing the public's attention.

Additionally, it is important to consider

seasonality and specific events that might interest your audience. For example, if you run a fashion blog, you could create content on spring trends or holiday outfits. Leveraging current events and trends will help you generate interest and engagement from your readers.

3. Use Engaging and Compelling Language

The way you express yourself in your online content is crucial to capturing your audience's interest. Use engaging, compelling, and easily understandable language to communicate effectively with your readers. Avoid overly technical terminology and try to maintain a conversational and friendly tone.

You can use copywriting techniques to create captivating titles and engaging descriptions that pique the audience's curiosity and encourage them to click and read your content. Additionally, make sure to provide useful and interesting information in the body of the text, maintaining a balance between entertainment and information.

4. Use Diverse Formats

To maintain the long-term interest of your audience, it is important to diversify the formats of your online content. Besides classic written articles, you can create videos, podcasts, infographics, webinars, interactive surveys, and much more. This will allow you to reach a broader audience and offer content that matches your readers' consumption preferences.

Different formats also allow you to express your creativity and provide a more engaging experience for your readers. For example, you can create video tutorials to explain complex concepts in a simple and intuitive way, or organize interactive webinars to engage your audience in real time. Experiment with different formats and monitor performance to understand what works best for your audience.

5. Offer Original and Unique Content

The key to attracting online interest is to offer original and unique content that stands out from the competition. Avoid copying or reusing existing web content and try to create something new and innovative that meets your audience's needs. Creating original content will help you build authority in your field and differentiate yourself from the competition.

To create unique content, you can leverage your experience and specific skills, proposing original insights and analyses on topics of interest to your audience. Additionally, you can involve experts and influencers in your industry to enrich your content with different perspectives and specialized insights.

6. Optimize for Search Engines (SEO)

To maximize the visibility of your online content and attract a wider audience, it is important to optimize your website or blog for search engines. Use specific and relevant keywords in the title, description, and text of your content to help search engines index and correctly position your site in search results.

Additionally, make sure you have a well-organized content structure, with titles, subtitles, and paragraphs that make the text easily readable for both search engines and your readers. Also, include internal and external links to related content to improve your site's authority and encourage user interaction.

7. Promote on Social Media Channels

Once you have created engaging online content for your blog or business, it is essential to promote it on social media channels to maximize visibility and audience interaction. Share your content on platforms like Facebook, Twitter, Instagram, LinkedIn, and Pinterest to reach a wider and more diverse audience.

Use captivating images and engaging descriptions to capture your followers' attention and encourage them to share your content. Interact with your audience through comments, likes, and shares to build trust and loyalty with your readers. Additionally, you can use advertising tools like Facebook Ads or Google AdWords to promote your content in a targeted and strategic way.

Creating engaging online content for a business or blog requires time, effort, and creativity, but the positive results you can achieve are truly rewarding. By following the tips and strategies described in this article, you will be able to create effective, engaging, and relevant content to attract and maintain the interest of your online audience. Remember to stay updated on the latest trends and constantly monitor your content's performance to optimize your strategy and achieve better results.

2. Understand Your Audience and Analyze Your Target

To succeed online, it is essential to have a clear understanding of your target audience. Understanding your target means knowing who the people interested in the content you produce are, what their interests and needs are, so you can create content that meets their expectations and captures their attention.

First of all, it is important to define who your target audience is. This process can be carried out through the analysis of demographic data such as age, gender, geographical location, income, and education. A more in-depth analysis of the audience can also involve defining interests, behaviors, habits, and consumption preferences. To get a clear picture of your audience, you can use tools like Google Analytics, Facebook Insights, online surveys, demographic and behavioral analysis of website or blog visitors.

Once you have identified your target audience, you can start creating content that captures their interest and generates engagement. Here are some tips on how to create engaging content for a blog or online business:

1. Personalize the content: Use demographic and behavioral data to personalize the content so that it is relevant to your target audience. For example, if your audience is primarily composed of women aged 25 to 35 interested in fashion, you can create content on fashion trends, style tips, and makeup tutorials.

2. Respond to the audience's needs and problems: Identify your audience's needs and problems and create content that helps them solve them. For example, if your audience is composed of university students interested in finding a job after graduation, you can create guides on how to write an effective resume, prepare for a job interview, and find internship opportunities.

3. Engage your audience: Engage your audience through surveys, open questions, contests, and online polls to better understand their interests and get feedback on already published content. This will help create a closer relationship with your audience and maintain high engagement.

4. Create original and unique content: To stand out from the competition and capture your audience's attention, it is important to create original, unique, and high-quality content. This can be done through researching new trends, developing unique insights, and using innovative formats such as videos, podcasts, and infographics.

5. Optimize for search engines: Use the best SEO practices to optimize your content so that it is easily findable by search engines. This includes using relevant keywords, well-optimized titles and meta descriptions, internal links, and high-quality backlinks.

6. Collaborate with influencers and brand ambassadors: Collaborate with influencers and brand ambassadors who have a similar audience to yours to reach new users and increase online visibility. These collaborations can be in the form of sponsorships, partnership collaborations, or joint content publishing.

7. Monitor content performance: Use web analytics tools to monitor content performance and understand which types of content work best with your audience. This will allow you to adapt your content strategy based on the results obtained and optimize future publications.

Understanding your target audience is essential to create engaging online content that can attract and engage the target audience. Using demographic, behavioral data, and interests, it is possible to personalize content, respond to the audience's needs, generate engagement, and increase online visibility. By following the suggestions described above and constantly monitoring content performance, it is possible to improve your content strategy and achieve positive long-term results.

3. Identify Needs, Interests, and Preferences

To create engaging online content for a business or blog, it is essential to identify the needs, interests, and preferences of your target audience. This step is crucial to ensure that the produced content can capture users' attention and maintain their interest over time.

To identify the needs, interests, and preferences of your target audience, you need to conduct thorough market research. This process can include collecting demographic data, analyzing users' online behaviors, and evaluating consumption trends in the reference sector. Additionally, it is important to actively involve your audience through surveys, interviews, or focus groups to better understand their needs and preferences.

Once the needs, interests, and preferences of your target audience have been identified, you can create engaging online content that aligns with this information. This way, you can ensure that the produced content meets your audience's needs and interests, thus increasing the likelihood of generating engagement and fostering user loyalty.

To create engaging online content, it is crucial to consider various aspects, including:

1. Relevance: The produced content must be relevant and useful for your target audience. It is important to talk about topics that interest readers and can address their specific needs.

2. Originality: To capture users' attention, it is essential to create original and unique content that stands out from the competition. This can be achieved through in-depth

research and analysis, as well as a creative and innovative approach to content production.

3. Variety: To maintain your audience's interest over time, it is important to vary the types of content produced. This can include informative articles, video tutorials, infographics, podcasts, interactive surveys, etc. The variety of content allows satisfying different user preferences and maintaining high engagement.

4. Interactivity: Actively involving your audience is crucial to create an emotional connection and establish a relationship of trust. You can use interactivity tools such as surveys, quizzes, contests, and live streaming to encourage user participation and make them an integral part of the content creation process.

5. Personalization: Adapting content to users' personal preferences is a great way to increase interest and engagement. Using segmentation tools to offer personalized content based on individual users' preferences can significantly increase the effectiveness of content marketing strategies.

6. SEO: To ensure that your content is easily findable online, it is essential to optimize it for search engines. Using relevant keywords, properly structuring content, and including internal and external links can help improve search engine rankings and increase online visibility.

Creating engaging online content for a business or blog is crucial to attract and retain the attention of the target audience. This process requires thorough market research and the ability to adapt content to users' specific needs. By following the above-described suggestions and maintaining a creative and innovative approach to content production, it is possible to increase audience engagement and achieve online marketing goals.

4. Define Content Goals

When creating online content for a business or blog, it is crucial to clearly define the content goals. Content goals are guidelines that help you create clear, consistent, and relevant messages for your target audience. These goals can vary depending on the type of business or blog you are running and the objective you want to achieve with your content.

The first step in defining content goals is to understand your target audience. Who are your ideal readers or customers? What are their interests, needs, and desires? What do they expect to find in your content? Answering these questions will help you create content that is truly relevant and interesting for your audience.

Once you have identified your target audience, you can start defining your content goals. Here are some common goals you might want to achieve with your content:

1. Educate your audience: One of the main goals of content is to educate your audience on specific topics. For example, if you have a cooking blog, you might want to educate your readers on cooking techniques, ingredients, and recipes. Creating informative and high-quality content will allow you to position yourself as an expert in your field and provide added value to your readers.

2. Engage your audience: Another important goal is to engage your audience and create interaction with them. You can do this by organizing surveys, asking them to share their opinions in the comments, or encouraging them to participate in contests and games. Keeping your audience engaged is essential to maintain interest in your content and encourage reader loyalty.

3. Generate traffic: If you have an online business, one of the main content goals might

be to generate traffic to your website or blog. To do this, it is important to create search engine optimized (SEO) content and promote it through social media and other online platforms. This way, you can attract more visitors to your site and increase your online visibility.

4. Build brand awareness: Another content goal might be to build brand awareness and introduce your brand to the public. You can do this by creating content that reflects your brand's values, mission, and personality and promoting it in a way that makes it visible to as many people as possible.

5. Generate leads and conversions: Finally, a key content goal is to generate leads and conversions for your business. You can do this by providing users with informative and valuable content and inviting them to leave their contact details to receive more information or offers. This way, you can create a database of potential customers interested in your products or services and

convert them into sales.

Once the content goals are defined, it is important to carefully plan the type of content to create and how to promote it to achieve your goals. You can use tools like an editorial plan and an article calendar to plan content in advance and ensure consistency and coherence in your messaging.

Additionally, it is important to constantly monitor your content's performance and analyze the data to understand what works and what doesn't. You can use tools like Google Analytics to track your site's traffic, user dwell time, and conversions to evaluate your content's effectiveness and make any necessary changes based on the results obtained.

Defining content goals is crucial to creating successful online content and achieving your marketing and communication goals. Identifying your target audience, establishing specific and measurable goals, planning content carefully, and monitoring performance are key steps to creating engaging and relevant content for your audience and achieving positive results for your online business.

5. Purpose of Communication and Key Message

In a world where digital communication has taken on an increasingly central role in our lives, it is crucial to understand how to create engaging online content for a business or blog. The main goal of this communication is to attract the audience's attention and engage them meaningfully, creating a bond that can lead to positive results for the business or blog in question.

The key message to convey in this context is the need to create original, interesting, and relevant content for your target audience. This can be achieved through a series of strategies and techniques aimed at capturing users' attention and maintaining their interest over time.

To create engaging online content for a business or blog, it is important to first identify who your target audience is. Knowing the demographic characteristics, interests, and consumption habits of your potential readers is essential to create content that can meet their needs and attract them.

Once you have identified your target audience, it is important to establish what are the most interesting topics for them and on which you intend to focus the content of your blog or online business. This can be done through market analysis, surveys, or simply observing online trends and the most popular discussions on social media.

Another effective strategy for creating engaging online content is to constantly update your site or blog with new articles, videos, or podcasts. This not only helps maintain the audience's attention but can also favor a better search engine ranking, thus increasing the visibility of the business or blog.

Additionally, it is important to use a variety of content formats to maintain users' interest and offer them a more engaging experience. For example, you can use images, videos, infographics, or quizzes to make the content more interesting and captivating.

Another important strategy for creating engaging online content is to actively interact with your audience through comments, private messages, or discussions on social media. This not only helps create a closer bond with users but can also provide insights and ideas for new content to create.

Finally, to create engaging online content, it is essential to constantly monitor the performance of your content. Using traffic and social media analysis tools can help understand which types of content work best and which can be improved, thus allowing you to optimize your online communication strategy.

Creating engaging online content for a business or blog is a complex process that requires time, dedication, and creativity. However, by following the right strategies and techniques, it is possible to achieve excellent results, attract new users, and retain those already acquired, thus creating a solid foundation for the growth and success of the business or blog online.

6. Call to Action

In recent years, with the explosion of the digital world, it has become increasingly important to have a strong and interesting online presence to attract potential customers. One of the best ways to do this is to create engaging content that involves your audience and drives them to act, in other words, create a "Call to Action."

But what exactly does "Call to Action" mean? A Call to Action is an invitation to perform a specific action, which can be a purchase, a registration, a social media share, etc. In simple terms, it is a way to guide your users towards a specific goal.

But how can you create an effective Call to Action for your blog or online business? Here are some useful tips to do so:

1. Know your audience: First of all, it is

important to know who your target audience is and what their needs and interests are. Only then can you create content that is truly relevant to them and drives them to act.

2. Choose the right tone of voice: When it comes to creating a Call to Action, it is important to choose the right tone of voice. It must be persuasive and engaging, but also clear and direct. Avoid overly complicated or ambiguous phrases, try to be concise and convincing.

3. Use visual elements: Visual elements like images and videos can increase the effectiveness of a Call to Action. Use them to capture your audience's attention and make the invitation more appealing.

4. Offer an incentive: Often, people are more inclined to act if there is something in return. Offer them an incentive, such as a discount or a gift, in exchange for the action you want them to take.

5. Create a sense of urgency: People are more likely to act if they feel a sense of urgency. Use phrases like "Limited offer" or "Last chance" to push your audience to act immediately.

6. Test and monitor the results: Finally, it is important to test different Calls to Action and monitor the results to understand what works best with your audience. Use tools like Google Analytics to track conversions and make any necessary adjustments.

Examples of effective Calls to Action could be:

- "Subscribe to our newsletter and receive a 10% discount on your next purchase"

- "Share this post on social media and get a chance to win a trip"

- "Book your appointment now and save 20% on the treatment"

- "Click here to download our free guide and

discover the secrets of online success"

Remember that an effective Call to Action must always be clear, persuasive, and focused on the value you offer to your audience. Don't be afraid to experiment and test different strategies to find the one that works best for you. With a bit of creativity and commitment,

you will surely be able to create engaging content that will involve your audience and drive them to act.

7. Choose the Most Suitable Content Formats

Choosing the most suitable content formats for your blog or online business can make a difference in audience engagement and the success of your content marketing strategy. Each format has its pros and cons, and the choice depends on the nature of the content you want to share, the target audience, and the goals you want to achieve.

In this article, we will explore the most popular content formats: text, images, video, infographics, and podcasts, and give you tips on how to use them effectively to engage your audience and increase your online business's visibility.

Text:

Text is one of the most traditional and still very effective content formats for communicating complex and in-depth information. Blog posts, guides, and informative articles are great for positioning yourself as an expert in your field and offering valuable content to your audience. Additionally, search engines favor high-quality textual content, so text is essential to improve your website's search engine ranking.

To create interesting textual content, it is important to maintain a conversational and accessible tone, use short and readable paragraphs, and enrich the text with captivating titles, bullet points, and internal and external links. Additionally, it is crucial to optimize the text for search engines by including relevant keywords and writing catchy meta descriptions.

Images:

Images are essential to capture the audience's attention and make content more appealing and memorable. Images can be used to illustrate complex concepts, evoke emotions, and improve engagement and social media sharing. It is important to choose high-quality images that match your brand identity's tone and style and optimize them for the web to ensure fast loading times.

To integrate images into your content, you can use original photos taken by your business, custom graphics, funny memes, infographics, and more. Make sure to respect copyright and only use images you have usage rights for.

Video:

Video is one of the most engaging and popular content formats on the internet. Videos can be used to tell stories, show products in action, share tutorials and interviews, and create fun and viral content. Videos are ideal for emotionally and persuasively engaging the audience and can help improve your website's search engine visibility.

To create successful videos, it is important to carefully plan the content, use good lighting and clear audio, edit accurately, and include clear calls to action to engage the audience. You can publish your videos on platforms like YouTube, Facebook, Instagram, and TikTok and share them on your website and social media to maximize their reach.

Infographics:

Infographics are a combination of text and images that allow presenting complex information clearly, visually, and appealingly. Infographics are ideal for sharing statistics, data, and processes in a visually captivating way and can be easily shared and embedded in blog posts, presentations, and marketing strategies.

To create memorable infographics, it is important to choose an attractive and intuitive design, use colors and typography consistent with your brand identity, and include accurate and relevant data. You can use online tools like Canva, Piktochart, and Venngage to easily create high-quality infographics even without advanced graphic design knowledge.

Podcasts:

Podcasts are audio content that can be streamed or downloaded on mobile devices to be listened to anytime and anywhere. Podcasts are ideal for sharing interviews, stories, in-depth discussions, and educational content and can help you build a more personal relationship with your audience.

To create successful podcasts, it is important to plan the content, use good audio equipment, maintain a regular publication schedule, and promote your episodes on social media and your website. You can host your podcast on platforms like Anchor, Spotify, and Apple Podcasts and share it on blogs and social media to increase its visibility and audience.

Choosing the most suitable content formats depends on the nature of the content you want to share, the target audience, and the goals you want to achieve. Using a combination of text, images, videos, infographics, and podcasts can help you effectively engage the audience, improve your online business's visibility, and stand out from the competition. Experiment with different content formats and monitor the results to understand what works best for your audience and adapt your content marketing strategy accordingly.

8. Create an Editorial Plan

Creating an editorial plan is a fundamental step in effectively managing the online presence of a business or blog. A well-structured editorial plan allows you to plan the content to be published, defining objectives, themes, publication frequency, and distribution methods. This way, it is possible to maintain consistency between the different content, creating a narrative that engages the audience and encourages interaction.

The first step in creating an editorial plan is to define the goals you want to achieve with your online presence. Goals can vary: increasing brand visibility, generating traffic to the site, obtaining conversions, improving search engine rankings, or building audience loyalty. Once the goals are defined, you can identify the themes to focus on to achieve them. The themes must be consistent with the business or blog and interesting for the target audience.

Once the themes are identified, you can move on to content planning. It is important to define an editorial line that clarifies the tone of voice to use, the graphic style, and the type of content to publish. It is also appropriate to establish a publication frequency, trying to maintain consistency over time. It is advisable to create an editorial calendar to schedule the content to be published and the related publication dates.

Content can be of different types: in-depth articles, practical guides, reviews, interviews, videos, infographics. It is important to vary the formats to maintain the audience's interest and encourage social media sharing. It is also possible to plan evergreen content, i.e., content that remains relevant and generates traffic over time, and timely content that deals with trending topics.

A fundamental aspect in creating an editorial plan is keyword research. Keywords allow optimizing the content for search engines, improving the site's ranking in user searches.

It is possible to use tools like Google Keyword Planner to identify the most relevant keywords for the treated topics. It is also advisable to constantly monitor the performance of the published content, evaluating which topics were most appreciated by the audience and which can be improved.

To increase audience interaction, it is important to engage users through comments, surveys, contests, open questions. It is also possible to collaborate with influencers and sector experts to create valuable content and increase brand visibility. It is important to enhance the content through a social media and newsletter diffusion strategy, using advertising tools to increase content visibility.

Finally, it is essential to constantly monitor the results obtained through tools like Google Analytics. It is possible to evaluate the generated traffic, user behavior, and obtained conversions. Based on the collected data, it is possible to correct and optimize the editorial plan, updating the treated themes, content formats, used keywords. This way, it is possible to constantly improve the online presence and achieve the set goals.

Creating an editorial plan is an essential step to effectively manage the online presence of a business or blog. Thanks to the definition of objectives, themes, publication frequency, and content diffusion methods, it is possible to maintain consistency between the different content and create a narrative that engages the audience. Through constant analysis of results and continuous optimization of the editorial plan, it is possible to improve the online presence and achieve the set goals.

9. Publication Frequency and Topic Calendar

The publication frequency and topic calendar are two fundamental elements to create engaging online content for a business or blog. Ensuring a constant online presence with quality and relevant content is essential to maintain and increase the interest of your audience and achieve your marketing and communication goals.

Publication frequency refers to the regularity with which new content is published on your website, blog, or social media. This parameter varies according to needs and available resources, but it is important to maintain a certain consistency and constancy. Indeed, sporadic or irregular content publication can lead to a loss of audience interest and compromise your credibility.

The topic calendar, on the other hand, consists of strategically organizing the themes and content you intend to cover over a certain period of time. This allows you to plan content creation in advance, ensuring greater consistency and cohesion between the various articles and posts. Additionally, it helps to keep the focus on topics relevant to your target audience and make the most of opportunities offered by events and anniversaries related to your sector or business.

To create an effective topic calendar, it is important to consider several factors and follow some key steps:

1. Define communication and marketing goals: first of all, it is essential to have clear goals you want to achieve with your content marketing strategy. Whether it is increasing brand visibility, generating qualified leads, or improving engagement with your audience, it is important that the topics covered are in line with these goals.

2. Know your target audience: to create engaging online content, it is essential to thoroughly know your target audience. It is important to understand their interests, needs, problems, and passions to create content that resonates with them and arouses their interest.

3. Conduct market research and competitor analysis: to better understand the context in which you operate and identify opportunities and challenges in your sector, it is useful to conduct thorough market research and analyze competitor strategies. This allows identifying sector trends, hot topics to cover, and gaps to fill with your content.

4. Create a list of main topics and categories: once all the necessary information is gathered, you can proceed to create a list of main topics and categories to cover in your content. These can include a variety of themes related to your business, sector, and audience passions, ensuring a certain diversity and freshness in the published content.

5. Plan publication frequency and topic distribution: precisely establishing the publication frequency of your content is fundamental to maintaining consistent audience interest and improving your online visibility. It is also important to plan the distribution of topics over time to ensure comprehensive coverage of the main themes and stimulate audience engagement.

6. Monitor and evaluate results: finally, it is important to constantly monitor content performance and evaluate the results obtained to make any necessary corrections and improvements to your content marketing strategy. Analyzing engagement, traffic, and conversion metrics helps understand what works and what doesn't, and optimize communication strategies.

Creating engaging online content for a business or blog requires accurate planning, research, and analysis, but it can bring significant benefits in terms of visibility, credibility, and engagement. Following a well-structured topic calendar and maintaining a constant and coherent publication frequency are key tools to achieve your communication and marketing goals and capture the attention and loyalty of your target audience.

10. Content Structure

Creating engaging online content for a business or blog is of fundamental importance to attract and engage your target audience. The content structure plays a crucial role in this process, as it must be organized in a way that is interesting and engaging for readers. In this article, we will explore how to create an effective structure for online content that can capture the audience's attention and generate positive interactions.

1. Identify your target audience

The first step to creating engaging online content is to identify your target audience. It is essential to know who you want to reach with your content so that you can adapt the message and tone to the needs and interests of your audience. Before you start creating content, it is therefore important to conduct market research to understand who the potential readers are and what their needs and interests are.

2. Define content goals

Once you have identified your target audience, it is important to define the goals of the content you want to create. Goals can be multiple, such as increasing brand visibility, generating leads, or positioning yourself as an expert in a specific sector. Clearly defining content goals helps create focus and maintain consistency in the message you want to convey.

3. Choose content format

When it comes to creating online content, there are several formats to choose from. The most common ones include blog posts, articles, ebooks, videos, infographics, and podcasts. It is important to choose the format that best suits your target audience and content goals. For example, if your target audience consists mainly of people who prefer visual content, it might be more appropriate to create infographics or videos.

4. Create a captivating title

The title is the first element that the reader sees when they come across online content, so it is crucial that it is captivating and arouses interest. The title should be short, clear, and promising to capture the reader's attention and encourage them to read the rest of the content. You can use provocative titles, questions, numbers, or statistics to make the title more engaging.

5. Structure the content clearly and engagingly

Once a captivating title is created, it is important to structure the content clearly and engagingly. The content structure should include an introduction that presents the topic being covered, a central body where the various aspects of the topic are explored in-depth, and a conclusion that summarizes the main concepts and invites the reader to interact.

To make the content more readable and engaging, you can use short paragraphs, bullet points, titles, and subtitles that divide the text into easily identifiable sections. Additionally, it is important to use clear and accessible language, avoiding technicalities and jargon that might be difficult for the reader to understand.

6. Use multimedia content

To make online content more interesting and engaging, it is advisable to use multimedia content such as images, videos, infographics, or gifs. Multimedia content helps make the text more lively and captivating and can facilitate the understanding of the discussed concepts. Additionally, multimedia content can be a great opportunity to differentiate yourself from the competition and create unique and original content.

7. Include calls-to-action

To maximize the effectiveness of online content, it is important to include calls-to-action that invite the reader to take a specific action. Calls-to-action can vary depending on content goals, such as subscribing to a newsletter, downloading an ebook, sharing the content on social media, or contacting the company for more information.

Calls-to-action should be strategically placed within the content and should be clear and convincing. It is important that calls-to-action are consistent with the topic being covered in the content so that they seem natural and not forced.

The structure of online content plays a crucial role in the success of a business or blog online. Creating interesting and engaging content requires time and effort, but by following the above-described advice, it is possible to increase brand visibility and generate positive interactions with your target audience. The key to creating engaging online content is to know your target audience, define content goals, choose the most suitable format, create a captivating title, structure the content clearly and engagingly, use multimedia content, and include convincing calls-to-action.

11. Writing Engaging Content

Creating engaging content for a website, blog, or online business is essential to capture the audience's attention and keep them engaged. Clear and engaging language is the key to creating interesting content that can capture users' attention and make them stay on your site or blog. In this text, we will explore how to create engaging content using clear and engaging language for your online business.

First of all, it is important to clearly define the information you want to communicate. Defining the main theme of your site or blog and identifying your target audience will help you create relevant and targeted content. Once you have defined your target audience, you can start creating content that can respond to their needs and interests.

A good way to create engaging content is to use simple, clear, and engaging language. Avoid technicalities and complicated wordings that might confuse your readers. Try to use informal and colloquial language that can make your content easily understandable and accessible to everyone.

Additionally, it is important to use an empathetic and engaging tone to create an emotional bond with your readers. Show yourself to be authentic and passionate about your topics, and you will be able to transmit enthusiasm and interest to your readers.

An effective technique to create engaging content is to use stories and metaphors. Telling engaging stories and using metaphors can make your content more memorable and engaging. Stories can create an emotional bond with your readers and keep them engaged in your message.

Additionally, it is important to use high-quality images and videos to enrich your content and make it more captivating. Images and videos can capture your readers' attention and make your content more interesting and engaging.

Finally, it is important to create a clear and well-organized structure for your content. Use captivating titles and subtitles to guide your readers through your content and make reading easier. Use bullet points and short paragraphs to make your content more readable and encourage scanning by your readers.

Creating engaging content for your online business requires using clear and engaging language, being empathetic and passionate about your topics, using stories and metaphors, enriching your content with high-quality images and videos, and creating a well-organized and clear structure. By following these guidelines, you will be able to create interesting content that will capture your readers' attention and keep them engaged on your site or blog.

12. Use Effective Titles and Subtitles

How to Create Engaging Online Content for a Business or Blog

In recent years, creating online content has become one of the most effective strategies to promote a business or blog. However, to succeed in this field, it is crucial to know how to create engaging content that attracts and involves your target audience. In this article, we will explore some techniques and strategies to create quality content that can generate interest and engagement online.

1. Know Your Target Audience

Before creating any type of online content, it is essential to know your target audience. It is important to understand who your readers are, what their interests, needs, and preferences are. Only this way can you create engaging content that can arouse their interest and involvement.

To know your target audience, you can use tools like Google Analytics to analyze visitor behavior on your website, social media to understand which types of content are most appreciated, and online surveys to collect feedback directly from your readers.

Once this information is acquired, it will be easier to create targeted content that meets your target audience's needs and preferences.

2. Choose the Right Topics

Once you have identified your target audience, it is important to strategically choose the content topics. To do this, you can use tools like Google Trends to identify current search trends and find topics of interest for your audience.

Additionally, you can also monitor competitors to understand which topics work best in your sector and get inspired by them to create original and quality content.

It is also important to diversify content topics, trying to cover a wide range of themes that can interest your target audience. This way, you can keep readers' interest alive and attract new visitors to your website or blog.

3. Create Original and Quality Content

One of the fundamental rules to succeed in creating online content is to create original and quality material. It is important to avoid copying content from other websites or blogs and try to offer added value to your readers through unique and informative content.

To create quality content, it is essential to conduct thorough research on the topic to be covered, consult authoritative sources, and verify the information before publishing it online. Additionally, it is also important to take care of the content form, using clear and engaging language and including multimedia elements like images, videos, or infographics to make the content more interesting and engaging.

4. Use the Right Distribution Platforms

Once the content is created, it is crucial to distribute it through the right online platforms to reach your target audience. It is important to choose the most suitable distribution channels for your sector and business and use tools like social media, search engines, or newsletters to promote your content.

Additionally, it is also important to optimize content for search engines using the right keywords and creating catchy titles and informative meta tags. This way, you can increase your content's online visibility and attract new visitors to your website or blog.

5. Keep Content Updated and Relevant

To keep your readers' interest alive and succeed in creating online content, it is essential to keep your content updated and relevant over time. It is important to monitor current search trends, review and update old content, and create new content in line with your audience's needs and preferences.

Creating engaging online content for a business or blog requires a strategic approach that considers various factors, including researching relevant and

 interesting topics for your target audience, taking care of the visual presentation of content, and using effective promotion and distribution tools.

To start, it is essential to identify your target audience and understand what their interests, needs, and preferences are in terms of content.

This step is crucial to create content that resonates with the audience and can capture their attention and engagement.

Once the target audience is identified, you can move on to the research phase of the topics to cover. It is important to choose topics that are relevant to the sector of the business or blog and that can provide useful and interesting information to the audience. You can use keyword research tools like Google Keyword Planner or SEMrush to identify the most searched topics online and understand current trends.

Additionally, you can also involve your audience in content creation by asking for feedback and suggestions directly from readers and creating content based on their requests and opinions.

Creating engaging online content for a business or blog can be a challenge, but with the right strategies and techniques, it is possible to attract and engage your target audience. Knowing your audience, choosing the right topics, creating original and quality content, using the right distribution platforms, and keeping content updated and relevant are just some of the fundamental steps to follow to succeed in creating online content.

By following these guidelines and implementing the right strategies, it is possible to create engaging content that can generate interest and engagement online, increase the visibility of your business or blog, and attract new visitors to your website.

13. Include Visual Elements to Make the Text More Appealing

Once the topics to be covered are chosen, it is crucial to take care of the visual presentation of the content. An attractive design and quality graphics can make a difference in making content more inviting and appealing to the audience. You can use design tools like Canva or Adobe Spark to create engaging images and graphic visualizations of data that can enhance content.

Additionally, it is important to consider text formatting and content structure. It is advisable to use short paragraphs, subtitles, and bullet points to facilitate reading and understanding of content. It is also important to include visual elements like images, videos, or infographics to make content more interesting and engaging for the audience.

Finally, to promote and spread content online, it is essential to use effective digital marketing strategies. It is possible to use social media to share content and interact with the audience, leveraging the power of visual storytelling to increase engagement and reach. Additionally, it is important to optimize content for search engines (SEO) to improve online visibility and attract organic traffic to your site.

Creating engaging online content for a business or blog requires a combination of strategic planning, creative execution, and effective promotion. By knowing your audience, defining clear goals, choosing the right content formats, and leveraging visual elements, you can create compelling content that captures the attention of your target audience and drives positive interactions. With continuous analysis and optimization, you can refine your content strategy and achieve your online marketing goals.

14. Optimizing Web Content: Using Relevant Keywords

Creating high-quality web content is essential to attract traffic to your site or blog and achieve the best possible search engine ranking. In this context, optimizing web content plays a crucial role, as it maximizes online visibility and reaches a wider audience.

One of the most effective strategies for optimizing web content is the use of relevant keywords. Keywords are terms or phrases that users type into search engines to find information on a specific topic. Choosing the right keywords is fundamental for ranking well on search engines and attracting visitors interested in your content.

To identify relevant keywords for your sector or niche market, it is important to conduct thorough market research and analyze user search trends. Several tools and software can help identify the most searched and used keywords by users, such as Google Keyword Planner, SEMrush, Ahrefs, and Moz Keyword Explorer.

Once you have identified the most relevant keywords for your content, it is important to use them strategically within the text. Keywords should naturally and coherently appear in the title, headers, subheaders, and body of the text. It is important to avoid excessive keyword stuffing, as this can penalize the content in the eyes of search engines.

Besides keywords, it is important to create high-quality and relevant content for users. Content should be original, interesting, informative, and useful for the target audience. It is advisable to enrich content with images, videos, infographics, charts, and other multimedia elements to make it more attractive and engaging.

Furthermore, it is essential to keep content updated and regularly publish new articles and posts on your site or blog. Search engines favor websites that consistently produce fresh and relevant content, so it is important to create an editorial strategy and regularly publish new content to maintain the attention of both users and search engines.

In addition to publishing new content, it is important to optimize existing content on your site or blog. You can improve existing content by correcting errors, updating information, and adding new multimedia elements. This will enhance the overall quality of the site and increase its visibility on search engines.

Another effective strategy for optimizing web content is to actively promote your content on social media and other online platforms. Sharing your articles and posts on social media increases the visibility of your site, broadens your audience, and drives traffic to your site or blog. Moreover, social media sharing can enhance your site's search engine ranking, as links from social media are considered a positive signal by Google's algorithms.

Finally, it is important to constantly monitor your content's performance and analyze the results obtained. Using traffic and conversion analysis tools, such as Google Analytics, allows you to evaluate the effectiveness of your optimization strategies and make any necessary corrections or improvements. Analyzing traffic, engagement, and conversion metrics helps understand which content works best and which can be further optimized to maximize results.

Optimizing web content through the use of relevant keywords, producing high-quality content, and actively promoting on social media is fundamental to attracting qualified visitors, improving search engine ranking, and generating value for your online business. By following these strategies and constantly monitoring the results obtained, it is possible to create a successful online presence and achieve tangible long-term results.

15. Optimizing Content Structure for Search Engine Ranking

In recent years, optimizing content for search engine ranking has become increasingly important for businesses aiming to increase their website visibility and attract more visitors. Creating engaging online content for a business or blog is essential to capture the audience's attention and achieve a high search engine ranking.

First of all, it is important to understand the goals of your website and business. You need to identify your target audience, understand their interests and needs, and create content that answers their questions and solves their problems.

Once you have defined your target audience, proceed with analyzing the most relevant keywords for your industry. Keywords are crucial for search engine ranking and should be integrated naturally into the content, without forcing or excessive repetition.

To create high-quality content that interests your audience, follow these fundamental steps:

1. **Research and Analyze Your Target Audience:** Understand who your readers are and what they search for online. Use tools like Google Analytics to analyze user behavior on your site and study search trends to understand the most searched topics in your industry.

2. **Create Original and Quality Content:** Provide useful and interesting information for your audience. Create guides, tutorials, reviews, and informative content that can answer readers' questions and meet their needs.

3. **SEO Optimization:** Once you have identified the most relevant keywords,

optimize your content for search engines. This means naturally integrating keywords into titles, subtitles, and the text. Pay particular attention to the meta description and images, including descriptive and relevant alt text.

4. **Link Building:** Create internal links between the pages of your website and obtain quality links from other websites. This will improve your site's authority in the eyes of search engines and enhance its ranking in search results.

5. **Monitor and Analyze Results:** Monitor content performance and analyze the results. Use tools like Google Search Console and Google Analytics to track organic traffic, keyword rankings, and page performance.

Creating engaging online content for a business or blog requires time, commitment, and expertise. It is important to be consistent and regularly update content to maintain audience interest and improve search engine ranking.

To optimize content structure for search engine ranking, it is essential to create high-quality content, optimized for keywords, and provide useful and interesting information for your target audience. By following SEO best practices and suggestions, you can improve your website's visibility and attract more visitors interested in your products or services.

16. Facilitating Social Media Sharing

Sharing content on social media is crucial to increase the visibility of a business or blog online, reach a wider audience, and boost user engagement. However, it is not enough to simply share content; it is necessary to create interesting and high-quality content to attract users' attention and encourage them to interact with your brand. In this article, we will explore how to create engaging online content to facilitate social media sharing.

1. Know Your Target Audience

Before creating content for social media, it is essential to know your target audience. Who are your followers? What are their interests, needs, and preferences? Which social media platforms do they use the most? Answering these questions will allow you to create more targeted content and, consequently, more interesting content for your audience.

2. Define Clear Objectives

Before creating content, it is important to establish clear and measurable objectives. What do you want to achieve by sharing your content on social media? Increase traffic to your website? Increase the number of followers? Increase sales? Boost user engagement? Defining objectives will help you create more effective content and evaluate your performance.

3. Create Valuable Content

To facilitate the sharing of your content on social media, it is essential to create valuable content for your audience. Content should be interesting, informative, useful, and original. You can create guides, tutorials, videos, infographics, podcasts, surveys, quizzes, etc. The important thing is to create content that meets your followers' needs and interests. Additionally, it is important to ensure the quality of the content, both textually and visually.

4. Use a Content Marketing Strategy

To create engaging online content, it is essential to use a content marketing strategy. This means creating an editorial plan, setting publication schedules, choosing the most suitable formats, creating evergreen content, and promoting content across various social media platforms. Moreover, it is important to monitor campaign results and make any necessary adjustments based on feedback received.

5. Engage Your Audience

To facilitate the sharing of your content on social media, it is important to engage your audience. You can ask questions, seek opinions, invite your followers to participate in surveys or quizzes, organize contests and giveaways, ask them to share your posts, etc.

The key is to create a dialogue with your audience and encourage interaction.

6. Use Hashtags Strategically

Hashtags are essential to increase the visibility of your content on social media. You can use hashtags to group your content into specific categories, increase your visibility in user searches, participate in specific conversations, and boost user engagement. It is important to use hashtags strategically, choosing those most relevant to your content and not overusing them.

7. Collaborate with Influencers and Brand Ambassadors

Collaborating with influencers and brand ambassadors can help increase the visibility of your content on social media. Influencers and brand ambassadors can share your content with their audience, increase your visibility, and attract new followers to your brand. It is important to choose influencers and brand ambassadors who align with your business values and goals.

8. Monitor and Analyze Results

To evaluate the effectiveness of your content marketing strategies, it is important to monitor and analyze campaign results. Use tools like Google Analytics, Facebook Insights, Instagram Analytics, Twitter Analytics, etc., to track website traffic, follower numbers, user engagement, and more. Based on the data collected, you can make any necessary adjustments to your strategy to achieve better results.

In conclusion, facilitating the sharing of content on social media is crucial to increase the visibility of your business or blog online. To create engaging online content, it is important to know your target audience, define clear objectives, create valuable content, use a content marketing strategy, engage your audience, use hashtags strategically, collaborate with influencers and brand ambassadors, and monitor and analyze campaign results. By following these tips, you can create high-quality and engaging content for your audience, increase your visibility and user engagement, and achieve your online communication goals.

17. Measure and analyze results. Monitor content performance

Measuring and analyzing results is a crucial phase in the process of creating online content for a business or blog. It's important to understand which content resonates most with your audience, generates the most interactions, and contributes to audience growth. This allows for optimizing the content marketing strategy to maximize outcomes.

Monitoring content performance requires using analytics tools such as Google Analytics, which provides detailed data on website traffic, visitor engagement, and other insights useful for evaluating marketing campaign effectiveness. Knowing which Key Performance Indicators (KPIs) to monitor, such as visits, conversion rates, average time spent on page, and bounce rate, is crucial.

Once data is collected, it's essential to analyze it to understand what works and what doesn't.

For example, if certain types of content receive more shares and comments than others, focusing on similar content can be beneficial. Conversely, if certain topics show low audience interest, it's advisable to avoid them.

Creating engaging content for a business or blog involves understanding the target audience's needs, desires, and problems. This understanding is essential for producing relevant and valuable content that encourages meaningful engagement and interaction.

Before creating content, thorough research into industry trends and the interests of the target audience is necessary. Understanding the most sought-after and discussed topics online helps create current and relevant content. Additionally, considering SEO requirements is important for optimizing content for search engines.

Another effective strategy for creating

engaging content is involving the audience through surveys, open-ended questions, and interest tests. Directly asking the audience about topics they want to see covered on the blog or social media can guide the creation of targeted and relevant content. It's also crucial to listen and respond to reader comments and feedback to understand their preferences.

Content diversity is another critical aspect to consider. Offering a mix of content types such as in-depth articles, video tutorials, infographics, podcasts, and more provides a broader range of options for the audience to consume and increases engagement.

To measure and analyze the results of created content, using key metrics such as visits, bounce rate, average time spent on page, social media shares and comments, and conversion rates is essential. These metrics provide valuable insights for evaluating content effectiveness and making necessary adjustments or improvements.

In addition to quantitative metrics, qualitative metrics such as audience feedback, reviews, and ratings are important. Listening to audience opinions helps understand what they appreciate about the content and what changes they would like to see. Monitoring user behavior on the website to identify the most visited pages and those that generate the most conversions is also beneficial.

Measuring and analyzing online content results is crucial for evaluating the effectiveness of the content marketing strategy and optimizing it to maximize outcomes. Using analytics and monitoring tools to gather detailed data on content performance and analyzing it helps understand what works best for the audience, leading to tangible results in promoting a business or online blog.

18. Analyzing Audience Engagement

Audience engagement is one of the most crucial aspects to consider when managing an online business or blog. It is essential to create content of interest that can engage the audience and prompt interaction with it. In this article, we will analyze some effective strategies to increase audience engagement and create content that can spark interest and involvement.

Firstly, it is important to understand who your target audience is and what their interests and needs are. This understanding is fundamental to creating content that can be relevant and interesting to them. Conducting market research and data analysis is helpful in gaining a better understanding of your users and what they are searching for online.

Once the target audience is identified, it is important to create original, creative, and high-quality content. Avoid publishing trivial and uninteresting content that will not elicit any kind of reaction from the audience. It is crucial to create unique and relevant content that can inform, entertain, or inspire users.

Another fundamental aspect to consider in increasing audience engagement is the consistency of posts. Maintaining a consistent posting frequency helps to keep the audience's interest alive and encourages them to return to the website or blog frequently. It is also important to maintain a consistent and recognizable style in your content to retain audience attention.

Another important element to consider is the use of social media to promote your content and stimulate audience engagement. Social media is a powerful tool for reaching a wide audience and increasing the visibility of your content. It is important to create content specifically for social media and use marketing strategies to increase audience interaction.

Another effective strategy to increase audience engagement is direct interaction with users. It is crucial to respond to user comments, involve them in discussions, and seek their opinions on specific topics. This approach helps to build a closer relationship with the audience and encourages active participation.

Monitoring audience engagement and analyzing data to understand what works and what doesn't is also crucial. There are various analytics tools that can help monitor audience interaction and identify the most appreciated content. It is important to use this data to optimize your content strategy and improve audience engagement.

Finally, it is important to continuously experiment and test new strategies to increase audience engagement. Staying updated on the latest trends in content marketing and adapting your strategy accordingly is important. Experimenting with new content formats, collaborating with influencers, or hosting live events can be excellent ways to stimulate audience interest and increase engagement.

Audience engagement is fundamental to the success of an online business or blog. Creating engaging content that can captivate the audience and encourage interaction is essential for maintaining audience interest and building an active and loyal community. Using effective strategies, such as analyzing the target audience, creating quality content, and promoting on social media, can help increase audience engagement and achieve your online marketing goals.

19. Making Any Changes and Improvements

To create compelling online content for a business or blog, it is important to have a well-defined digital marketing strategy and to stay informed about the latest industry trends. Here are some suggestions on how to make changes and improvements to create valuable content for your online business:

1. **Identifying Your Target Audience**: Before creating content, it is crucial to understand who your target audience is. This will enable you to create targeted and relevant content that can interest and engage your audience.

2. **Analyzing Competitors**: Studying your competitors can help you understand what works and what doesn't in the industry. By analyzing your competitors' content, you can draw inspiration and improve your content marketing strategies.

3. **Creating an Editorial Calendar**: To ensure a consistent production of quality content, it is advisable to create an editorial calendar to help plan your posts in advance. This way, you can ensure regular publishing and keep your audience engaged.

4. **Choosing the Right Channels**: In addition to your online blog, it is important to use other communication channels, such as social media, to promote your content and reach a wider audience. Make sure to choose channels that are most suitable for your industry and target audience.

5. **Creating Original and Valuable Content**: To attract and retain your readers, it is essential to create original and valuable content that addresses the needs and interests of your audience. Try to offer useful information, practical advice, and unique content that can set you apart from the competition.

6. **Using Images and Videos**: Visual elements are crucial for capturing the audience's attention online. Use high-quality images, short videos, and compelling graphics to make your content more interesting and engaging.

7. **Optimizing for Search Engines**: To increase the visibility of your online content, it is essential to optimize your website and posts for search engines. Use relevant keywords, create catchy titles, and make sure to include internal and external links to improve your search engine rankings.

8. **Monitoring Performance**: To evaluate the effectiveness of your content and make any necessary changes and improvements, it is important to continuously monitor the performance of your website and posts. Use web analytics tools to measure traffic, dwell time, and other key metrics to assess the success of your content.

9. **Engaging Your Audience**: Interacting with your readers is essential for creating a loyal and engaged online community. Respond to comments, ask for feedback, conduct surveys, and encourage your audience to share your content to enhance engagement and loyalty.

10. **Collaborating with Influencers and Partners**: To increase the visibility and engagement of your content, consider collaborating with influencers and industry partners. Organize contests, webinars, events, and other initiatives that can generate interest and engagement from your target audience.

To create compelling online content for a business or blog, it is essential to be creative, consistent, and informed about the latest industry trends. By following the above suggestions, you can improve your content marketing strategy and achieve positive results for your online business.

20. Tips for Creating Valuable Content

Creating valuable online content is essential for keeping readers interested and attracting new ones. There are many strategies that can be adopted to create quality content that is relevant to the target audience. Below are 40 tips for creating valuable online content for a business or online blog:

1. **Know Your Target Audience:** It's important to understand who your readers are and what they are interested in reading. This will help create relevant content that resonates with your target audience.

2. **Choose Relevant Topics:** Research trending topics in your industry and create current and interesting content on those topics.

3. **Be Authentic:** Transparency and authenticity are crucial for creating valuable online content. Being sincere and honest with

your audience helps build trust and credibility.

4. **Create Original Content:** Avoid copying or repurposing content already available online. Creating original content helps differentiate yourself from competitors and build a recognizable brand.

5. **Use High-Quality Images:** Images are crucial in online content. Use high-quality images to enhance content and capture readers' attention.

6. **Use Video and Graphics:** Videos and graphics can make content more engaging and memorable. Use them to explain complex concepts or add value to written content.

7. **Write Clearly and Concisely:** Use simple and direct language to make content easily understandable for your audience. Avoid complex technical terms or industry jargon.

8. **Use Bullet Points:** Divide content into bullet points or short paragraphs to make it easier to read and understand. This makes content more fluid and enjoyable to read.

9. **Use Catchy Headlines:** The headline is the first element that grabs readers' attention. Use catchy and interesting headlines to entice readers to read the rest of the content.

10. **Include Calls to Action:** Insert clear and direct calls to action to encourage readers to interact with the content, such as leaving a comment or sharing the content.

11. **Respond to Comments and Questions:** Be active in managing reader comments and questions. Respond promptly and courteously to create a positive relationship with your audience.

12. **Collaborate with Industry Professionals:** Involve experts and industry professionals to add value to your content and offer new perspectives to your audience.

13. **Maintain Publishing Frequency:** Keep a consistent publishing frequency to maintain audience interest and loyalty. Plan content to maintain a steady online presence.

14. **Use Social Media to Promote Content:** Share content on social platforms to increase visibility and reach a wider audience. Use hashtags and tags to expand reach.

15. **Monitor Content Performance:** Use analytics tools to monitor content performance and understand which types of content resonate best with your audience. Use this information to improve future content.

16. **Create Evergreen Content:** Create evergreen content that maintains its value over time and can be republished in the future. This helps maintain a steady flow of quality content.

17. **Conduct Interviews and Podcasts:** Engage experts and industry leaders to conduct interviews and podcasts. This adds value to your content and offers your audience new information and perspectives.

18. **Host Webinars and Online Events:** Host webinars and online events to engage your audience interactively and effectively. This helps create an active and loyal community.

19. **Use Infographics and Statistical Data:** Infographics and statistical data can make content more interesting and compelling. Use them to present complex information clearly and visually.

20. **Create In-Depth Content:** Create detailed and comprehensive content on specific topics to provide your audience with complete and detailed information. This helps position yourself as an expert in the field.

21. **Use Storytelling:** Use storytelling to create engaging and compelling content. Sharing personal stories or experiences can make content more emotional and memorable.

22. **Collaborate with Influencers:** Collaborate with industry influencers to increase content visibility and reach a wider audience. Influencers can help promote content and increase engagement.

23. **Create Guides and Tutorials:** Create practical guides and tutorials to help your audience solve problems or learn new skills. These types of content are highly appreciated and shared online.

24. **Maintain a Consistent Writing Tone:** Use a consistent and recognizable writing tone to create a recognizable brand identity. This helps create a consistent and professional online image.

25. **Respect SEO Guidelines:** Optimize content for search engines using appropriate keywords and respecting SEO rules. This helps improve online content visibility.

26. **Engage Audience with Surveys and Questionnaires:** Involve your audience in surveys and questionnaires to better understand their needs and preferences. Use this information to create more targeted and relevant content.

27. **Write Guest Posts on Other Blogs:** Write guest posts on other industry blogs to increase content visibility and reach a wider audience. This also helps build relationships with other industry professionals.

28. **Organize Contests and Giveaways:** Organize contests and giveaways to engage your audience and increase online engagement. These initiatives can create buzz around content and increase business visibility.

29. **Create Multimedia Content:** Use different content formats such as videos, podcasts, infographics, and presentations to make content more interesting and engaging. This helps cater to diverse audience preferences.

30. **Monitor Competitors:** Observe content published by competitors to understand what strategies work in the industry and gain inspiration to improve your own content.

31. **Collect Feedback and Reviews:** Ask your audience to leave feedback and reviews on your content to understand how it is perceived and what can be improved. Use this information to create more relevant and quality content.

32. **Participate in Online Forums and Communities:** Actively participate in industry forums and online communities to share your content and interact with your audience. This helps create a network of contacts and increase online visibility.

33. **Create a Newsletter:** Create a newsletter to regularly send interesting content to readers and keep them informed about the latest industry news. This is a great way to maintain direct contact with your audience.

34. **Be Creative and Innovative:** Experiment with new ideas and content formats to keep your audience interested and

curious. Being creative and innovative helps differentiate yourself from competitors and create unique and memorable content.

35. **Collaborate with Influencers:** Involve influencers and influential bloggers in the industry to promote your content and reach a wider audience. Influencers can help increase content visibility and online engagement.

36. **Create Seasonal Content:** Create content related to seasonal events or holidays to keep readers interested and offer thematic and current content. This helps create an emotional connection with the audience and increase engagement.

37. **Collaborate with Other Businesses:** Collaborate with other businesses and companies in the industry to create joint content and reach a wider audience. This helps expand online visibility and create strategic partnerships.

38. **Be Consistent and Patient:** Creating valuable online content takes time and effort. Being consistent in content publishing and patient in results helps build a loyal audience and improve online visibility over time.

39. **Observe Industry Trends:** Stay informed about the latest industry trends to create current and relevant content. Use this information to anticipate audience needs and offer quality content.

40. **Measure Results and Adapt:** Use analytics tools to measure content results and understand what works and what can be improved. Adapt your strategy based on results to create increasingly valuable content that interests your audience.

Creating valuable online content requires commitment, creativity, and strategy. Following these 40 tips can help create quality, relevant, and engaging content for your target audience, thereby contributing to building a positive and professional online image.

21. Glossary of Terms for Content Creators

A/B Testing: A method of testing two different versions of content (such as an email subject line or a landing page) to see which performs better with your audience.

Algorithm: A set of rules or calculations that determine how content is ranked or displayed on a particular platform (such as social media or search engines).

Analytics: Data and statistics that show how your content is performing, including metrics such as page views, click-through rates, and engagement.

Audience: The group of people you are creating content for, including their demographics, interests, and behaviors.

Blog: A website or online platform where an

individual or organization publishes written content on a regular basis.

Brand: The unique identity of a company or individual, including values, messaging, and visual elements that set them apart from others.

Call-to-Action (CTA): A prompt or instruction that encourages the audience to take a specific action, such as signing up for a newsletter or making a purchase.

Content Calendar: A schedule or plan that outlines when and where content will be published, including topics, formats, and deadlines.

Content Creator: Someone who produces and publishes digital content, such as videos, articles, social media posts, or podcasts.

Content Marketing: A strategic approach to creating and distributing valuable, relevant content to attract and engage a specific audience.

Content Management System (CMS): A software platform that helps create, manage, and organize digital content, such as WordPress or Joomla.

CPC (Cost Per Click): A metric that measures how much it costs to get a user to click on an ad or a link.

CPI (Cost Per Impression): A metric that measures how much it costs for an ad to be shown to a thousand users.

CPS (Cost Per Sale): A metric that measures how much it costs to generate a sale through advertising or marketing efforts.

CTA (Click-to-Action): A call-to-action that prompts the audience to click on a link or button to take a specific action.

CTR (Click-through Rate): A metric that measures the percentage of users who click on a link or ad after seeing it.

Dashboard: A visual display of key performance indicators (KPIs) and metrics that help monitor and track the performance of content campaigns.

Engagement: The level of interaction and participation from the audience, such as likes, comments, shares, and clicks.

Evergreen Content: Content that remains relevant and valuable over time, often being recycled and repurposed for multiple uses.

Freemium: A business model that offers basic

services for free, with premium features available as paid upgrades.

Growth Hacking: A marketing strategy that focuses on rapid experimentation and optimization to drive growth and expansion.

Hashtag: A word or phrase preceded by a pound sign (#) used on social media platforms to categorize content and make it searchable.

Impressions: The number of times an ad or piece of content is viewed, regardless of whether it is clicked on or not.

Influencer: Someone with a large and engaged following on social media, who can help promote products, services, or brands.

Keyword: A word or phrase that users type into a search engine to find relevant content, used for search engine optimization (SEO) purposes.

KPI (Key Performance Indicator): A measurable value that indicates how effectively a content campaign is achieving its objectives.

Lead Generation: The process of attracting and capturing potential customers' information for further marketing and sales efforts.

Metadata: Data that describes and gives information about other data, such as titles, descriptions, and tags used for content optimization.

Native Advertising: Paid content that is seamlessly integrated into a platform's user experience, such as sponsored articles or videos.

Organic Reach: The number of users who see

a piece of content without paid promotion or advertising.

Persona: A fictional representation of your ideal audience member, including characteristics, interests, and behaviors.

Podcast: An audio program or series that is available for streaming or download on digital platforms.

ROI (Return on Investment): A measure of the profitability of an investment, calculated as the ratio of net profit to the cost of the investment.

SEO (Search Engine Optimization): The process of optimizing content to increase its visibility and ranking on search engines.

SERP (Search Engine Results Page): The page that displays search engine results in response to a user query.

Social Media: Online platforms and websites that allow users to create and share content with their network, such as Facebook, Twitter, Instagram, and LinkedIn.

Target Audience: The specific group of people you want to reach with your content, based on demographics, interests, and behaviors.

UGC (User-Generated Content): Content created by users or customers, such as reviews, testimonials, or social media posts.

Video Marketing: The use of video content to promote products, services, or brands and engage with an audience.

Viral Marketing: A marketing strategy that seeks to create content that spreads rapidly and widely through social media and word-of-mouth.

Webinar: A live or pre-recorded seminar or presentation that is broadcasted over the internet for an audience to watch and engage with.

YouTube: A video-sharing platform where individuals and organizations can upload, share, and monetize video content.

Zero-Party Data: Data that users willingly provide to a company or brand, such as preferences, interests, or feedback, for a personalized experience.

This glossary provides a comprehensive list of terms and concepts that content creators should be familiar with to effectively create, distribute, and optimize digital content for their audience. By understanding these terms and incorporating them into their content strategy, creators can enhance their visibility, engagement, and ultimately, their success in the digital space.

Index

1. Introduction pg.4

2. Understand Your Audience and Analyze Your Target pg.12

3. Identify Needs, Interests, and Preferences pg.17

4. Define Content Goals pg.21

5. Purpose of Communication and Key Message pg.26

6. Call to Action pg.30

7. Choose the Most Suitable Content Formats pg.34

8. Create an Editorial Plan pg.41

9. Publication Frequency and Topic Calendar pg.45

10. Content Structure pg.50

11. Writing Engaging Content pg.56

12. Use Effective Titles and Subtitles pg.59

13. Include Visual Elements to Make the Text More Appealing pg.66

14. Optimizing Web Content: Using Relevant Keywords pg.68

15. Optimizing Content Structure for Search Engine Ranking pg.73

16. Facilitating Social Media Sharing pg.77

17. Measure and analyze results. Monitor content performance pg.83

18. Analyzing Audience Engagement pg.87

19. Making Any Changes and Improvements pg.91

20. Tips for Creating Valuable Content pg.95

21. Glossary of Terms for Content Creators pg.107

www.ingramcontent.com/pod-product-compliance
Lightning Source LLC
Chambersburg PA
CBHW072052230526
45479CB00010B/685